Lead with Levity

Strategic Humor for Leaders

SIGN-UP FOR FREE BONUS MATERIALS AT
WWW.KARYNBUXMAN.COM/LEADERSHIP

Lead with Levity
Karyn Buxman

Karyn Buxman, RN, MSN, CSP, CPAE

REGISTERED TRADEMARKS OF KARYN BUXMAN
WHAT'S SO FUNNY ABOUT...?®
HUMORx®

COVER PHOTO & DESIGN BY LAURA FORMAN

LEVITY WORKS PUBLISHING

SIGN-UP FOR FREE BONUS MATERIALS AT
WWW.KARYNBUXMAN.COM/LEADERSHIP

KARYN BUXMAN
858-603-3133
KARYN@KARYNBUXMAN.COM
WWW.KARYNBUXMAN.COM
WWW.FACEBOOK.COM/KARYNBUXMANSPEAKS
HTTPS://TWITTER.COM/KARYNBUXMAN
VIDEO TRAINING: WWW.AVANOO.COM/KARYNBUXMAN
WWW.LINKEDIN.COM/IN/KARYNBUXMAN

"Applied Humor as a Leadership Strategy":
The one class they didn't teach you
at Harvard Businss School."

~ Karyn Buxman

Table of Contents

"A sense of humor is
part of the art of leadership."

~ Dwight D. Eisenhower

1
Lead with Laughter

As I began the interview for my podcast, I looked at his boyish grin and into his playful eyes. "My guest today is a software engineer at Google. Chade-Meng Tan will be sharing his insights on *leading with levity.*"

"*Levity??* I thought you wanted to talk about *levitation,*" he said with a puzzled look on his face.

"Uh-oh," I thought. "This might be a disaster!"

Meng said, "I guess I'll have to throw out my notes!"

He then tipped back his head and roared with laughter. Perhaps I should mention that Meng is Google employee #107, and his position at Google is "Jolly Good Fellow."

"Leaders need to establish trust. Humor is a way of establishing trust," he said.

And I'll tell you from personal experience that Meng is a *master* of using humor; not only to build bonds of trust between us, but also to emphasize certain points and anchor them in my memory. Two weeks after our interview, Meng was nominated for the Nobel Peace Prize. He was honored for co-creating a global campaign he co-chairs called "1 Billion Acts of Peace." As a leader, he demonstrates that you can use humor as a way to change the world.

In *your* pursuit of better leadership skills you've already gathered an extensive set of tools: Focus. Vision. Values. Strategy. Tactics. Emotional intelligence. Goal-setting. Decision-making. Storytelling. Mentoring. Time management. Critical thinking. Cheese (how to move it.) Humor.

Humor??!

I've noticed that MBA programs rarely teach humor. And business books don't extol the benefits of humor in the corporate—or *any* organizational—setting. And that's too bad, because humor is a tool that enhances many of the *other* leadership tools that you use.

Humor enhances communication, bonds teams, improves retention, increases productivity, and improves profitability.

The effectiveness of humor used to be merely anecdotal. But now it's a scientifically proven fact that humor has significant physiological, social and psychological benefits. Over the past several decades neuroscientists and psychologists have been ferreting out the secrets of humor.

Research from Wharton, MIT, and London Business School reveal the practical benefits of humor in the workplace. Even "The Harvard Business Review" acknowledges that humor is an important leadership skill.

Let's begin by thinking about leaders who've influenced *you*. These might be teachers, bosses, politicians, spiritual leaders, friends or family members.

☛ A little exercise: Briefly write down some examples of humor used by friends or colleagues, or humorous conversations you've overheard, or instances of humor that you've *seen*: Funny signs, billboards, headlines, etc. Now, reflect on how they made you *feel*. Keep these examples in mind as we build your knowledge base and skill set throughout these pages.

As a leader, you need a *variety* of tools that will help you better guide, direct, and inspire others. These tools include your overall temperament and personal style; the manner in which you give guidance, instructions and reprimands; your ability to adapt your techniques to each person and each team you're addressing; the tone of your voice; the different styles of communications for one-on-one interactions, for small group meetings, and for large audience situations; your flexibility; your writing style; your confidence; your level of expertise, *and*—your use of humor.

I'm not talking about "telling jokes" here. The goal is *not* to turn you into a stand-up comedian! Humor as *entertainment* produces *enjoyment*—but humor as an intentionally-applied *strategy* produces *results*.

As you explore the insights and information in this little book, and then practice them in your everyday life and work environments, you will understand and experience the many benefits humor has to offer.

*

A Page for Doodling.

"The next best thing
to solving a problem is finding
some humor in it."

~ Frank A. Clark

2

Defining & Refining Humor

It was eight o'clock on a Monday morning when suddenly a rhythmic thumping noise brought my six-year-old to mind.

"Adam!" I called. No answer. "Adam!"

As I approached his bedroom I could *feel*, as well as *hear*, the "Whomp! Whomp! Whomp!"

I opened his door and there was my first grader—wearing nothing but his underwear and a big smile...jumping up and down on his bed...singing and dancing...swinging his school clothes over his head!

I lost it! *"What do you think you're doing?!"*

Adam stopped mid-jump, grinned a huge grin, and with the wisdom of Yoda, exclaimed, "Don't ya think getting dressed in the morning oughta be more *fun*?!"

My first response? "NO!!!"

My *second* response? "No more of Mommy's motivational tapes for you, young man!"

But moments later, my son's wisdom got through to me, and I realized he was *right*. Wouldn't it be marvelous if we all could have more fun while getting dressed, getting up, going to work . . . ? *It's not about what you're doing—it's about your attitude toward it.*

I began my research of applied and therapeutic humor in graduate school over three decades ago. My masters thesis researched the relationship between humor, health and communications. How do you *quantify* something like humor? Painstakingly and patiently! Before I could *measure* humor I had to *define* it.

Following is my definition of humor plus a couple of my *other* favorite definitions, from a couple of my good friends and colleagues in the field of appllied humor:

HUMOR IS...

*"Humor is a feeling of delight, wonder or
release that comes from surprise, perspective or
insight."*
~ Karyn Buxman

*"Humor is the intellectual mindset that
is expressed through the emotional feelings
of mirth and the physical expression of laughter."*
~ Steve Sultanoff, Ph.D.

*"Humor is a childlike perspective
in an otherwise serious adult reality."*
~ Joel Goodman, founder of The HUMOR Project

As a leader, it's important to keep in mind that what people find humorous is incredibly diverse. Strategically using this knowledge is what will differentiate you from a leader who is not only *entertaining*, but someone who is *powerful*.

✏ A little exercise: Today, start keeping a journal or an electronic file of things you find funny. Jokes, stories, cartoons, embarrassing moments, things you hear, bloopers in the media, videos, tweets...the list is practically endless! Tag your collection with helpful keywords so if you need an example for, say, resilience, or engagement, you can find it more easily. Keep your humor collection handy, as you'll need to tap into it later.

Everyone's sense of humor—whether it's yours or that of the people you lead—is as unique as their fingerprints. What people find funny is based on their life experiences, socialization, and emotional filters. In upcoming chapters you'll discover how to harness humor with confidence to attain success, significance and happiness.

*

A Page for Your Favorite Jokes.

_____
_____
_____
_____
_____
_____
_____
_____
_____
_____
_____
_____
_____

"Comedy is simply a funny way
of being serious."

~ PETER USTINOV

3
The Good, the Bad & the Ugly

☠

Over dinner, several board members of the organization for which I was speaking recounted their tales of humor at work. All of their stories—except one—was upbeat and made all of us laugh. The exception was Julia.

"In my previous job, I was the only woman at a mid-size advertising agency. My boss thought he was funny, but many of us found him to be crude and inappropriate. But he's the Boss, so what can you do?"

"Once, during a pitch to a client, I spoke up to share an idea. Boss held up his hand to 'shush' me, and then said to the client, 'Don't mind her. We call her by her Indian name, 'Running Commentary.' Everyone laughed. But I felt humiliated. This was a common occurrence. I called Boss on it a few times, but he always brushed me off. 'What's the matter, Julia? Can't you take a joke?' he would boom so the entire office could hear him. And since none of the other employees were brave enough to join me in standing up to him, nothing changed.

"I jumped ship as soon as I could."

Yes, humor can build people up—and it can also tear them down. Humor can be a double-edged sword. As a leader, you need to be aware of the Good, the Bad, and even the Ugly aspects of humor.

Humor, when used constructively, is a tool that can build people up, strengthen bonds and enhance communication. When used *negatively*, humor can intimidate and belittle others, destroy relationships and halt communication. In its most simplistic form, it's a question of "laughing WITH" someone, versus "laughing AT" someone. This might feel black-and-white, but I've observed that there's a bi-i-ig gray zone in between, depending on the intention of the sender.

As a leader, you'll want to be mindful of how you wield your humor, and help guide others to be more constructive with their humor, as well.

☞ A little exercise: Think of the last three humorous exchanges you've observed and write down a few words to describe each one. Then ask yourself: "What was the *intent* of the person making the humorous remark?" Was the humor to lift someone up? Or was is it to put someone down? Was the humor being used as a *tool*...or as a *weapon*?"

As a leader, it is important that you use positive humor intentionally. It will foster communication, strengthen relationships, and boost productivity. In upcoming chapters I'll cover a variety of ways to harness the power of humor, and do it constructively.

❋

"A person who belly-laughs
doesn't bellyache"

~ SUSAN THURMAN

4

"We'll Never Get Anything Done Around Here!"

"Humor in the workplace?! We'll never get anything done around here!" cried Henry, a CFO at a Fortune 500 company, shaking his head.

"Great!" I thought sarcastically. I was about to keynote for Henry's company meeting and already he was undermining my program—and his own goal—to improve the corporate culture.

I could tell by the look on his face just what he was afraid of: Unbridled joking around, horseplay and chaos! Aspiring Jim Carreys and Robin Williams's running rampant through the office hallways…A tidal wave of humor, jocularity, joking, jesting, chuckling, chortling, satire, farce, slapstick, gags, drollery, wise-cracking and—last but not least—puns!

Other members of the management team were still streaming into the ballroom for my presentation on "Humor and Leadership." But Henry, who had been with the organization 20 years, continued to spew negativity before his meeting even got started.

He continued…"This 'humor stuff' might work for *some* places, but here, if we don't keep our staff reigned in, their productivity's gonna go right down the !*?~#-!" [editor's note: replace "!*?~#-!" with "tubes"]

Henry assumed that humor in the workplace was about letting people have fun without any guidance at all. The fear of losing control was keeping him from allowing his staff, and himself, to experience the benefits that humor can bring to a corporate culture.

If you set high expectations for your staff while you stifle their sense of humor, your company culture can feel like, "Firings will continue until morale improves!" On the flip side, if you merely encourage humor in the workplace without being clear about expectations, company culture could disintegrate into disorder.

Research indicates that fun, upbeat, corporate cultures increase engagement, productivity and profits. The "Harvard Business Review" published a study demonstrating that happy employees have, on average, 31% higher productivity, 37% higher sales, and three times more creativity.

The key to effective humor in leadership is setting the *tone* for humor AND, at the same time, setting *high expectations*. It's pairing the two that will take your leadership to a higher level.

💭 A little exercise: Reflect on your expectations for those you're leading. Visualize and write down what your work environment would look like if those you led were fully engaged, enthused about their responsibilities, and having fun while they performed.

❂

Laughter rises out of tragedy,
when you need it the most, and
rewards you for your courage.

~ Erma Bombeck

5

Rx for Stress: Laughter

Beatings. Torture. Confinement. That was Captain Gerald Coffee's life for seven years as a prisoner of war in the infamous "Hanoi Hilton" during the Vietnam War.

During his captivity, he was held in a concrete cell ten inches wide, kept in leg irons, and fed food unfit for human consumption. Still, he found ingenious ways to cope, including humor.

Captain Coffee once saw half of a bug in a hunk of stale bread he was eating. He realized that he'd just swallowed the *other* half of the bug. Most people would be disgusted and angry. Coffee, however, was inspired to write a poem about it.

> *Little weevil in my bread*
> *I think I just bit off your head*
> *I see the place where you have bled*
> *The dough around it is all red*
> *But that's okay for now instead*
> *I know for sure you're really dead*
> *I wonder if your name was Fred*

Okay, so he's not Robert Frost. But that's not the point.

Coffee secretly relayed the poem to a fellow prisoner using a code they'd devised. Before he had finished communicating his opus, they began laughing so hard that they risked a beating if the guards had overheard them.

The stress-reducing effects of humor are so powerful that men would risk physical abuse just to share something funny with a colleague! I've studied humor for 25 years. I've heard and seen a lot. And I thought I knew all about the benefits and power of humor. But I stand in awe of Gerald Coffee, a U.S. Naval Captain, pilot and poet.

Stress can arise from *major life events* such as the death of a loved one or a divorce. It can come from *chronic strains,* such as living in an abusive relationship. Or it can appear from *occasional* strains, like getting a flat tire in rush-hour traffic.

In today's fast-paced culture, we're all faced with *some* degree of stress—cranky customers, irritable bosses, stubborn employees, budgets, deadlines, piles of paperwork. Experts estimate that stress-related ailments cost the U.S. $300 billion—every year!

The good news? Humor is a simple, cost-effective way to ward off many of the detrimental effects of stress.

Psychologically, humor acts as a positive coping mechanism, relieving anxiety and providing an emotional outlet for anger. Socially, humor helps us overcome isolation and loneliness. Physically, it provides healthy benefits to practically every major body system.

My friend and colleague Dr. Lee Berk says, "If we took what we now know about laughter and bottled it, it would require FDA approval."

☞ A little exercise: Carve out 20 minutes today for this exercise. Think of something that causes you stress, and on a scale of 1-to-10 rate your levels of anxiety and muscle tension. Write them down. Now watch or listen to 15 minutes of something that amuses you—a sitcom, internet videos of laughing babies, your favorite comedian. Then repeat your physical assessment and compare your results.

In his book, "Beyond Survival: Building on the Hard Times," Captain Coffee wrote, "Laughter sets the spirit free to move through even the most tragic circumstances. It helps us shake our heads clear, get our feet back under us and restore our sense of balance and purpose. Humor is integral to our peace of mind and ability to go beyond survival."

✳

Capture Your "Ah-Ha's" Here!

"The saving grace of humor is that
if you fail, no one is
laughing at you."

~ WHITNEY BROWN

6

"What If Nobody Laughs?!"

I sat at a table in the lounge, sharing a glass of wine with a dozen top-level financial planners. They appeared a lot more comfortable and a whole lot funnier than they had at the all-day meeting that had concluded a couple hours ago. I turned my attention to one of the senior VPs and said, "John, I never would've guessed you were so funny! Why didn't you show more of that when you were in front of the group today?"

He shrugged and said, "Sometimes I'm funny one-on-

one, but what if I'd said something to the group and nobody laughed?" His answer didn't surprise me. Even people who make a living at making people laugh are reluctant to throw out a funny line only to hear crickets in return.

Comics like Jimmy Fallon, Tina Fey, and Louis CK have all bit the big one at one point or another. There's even a YouTube channel called, "Worst I Ever Bombed."

I've interviewed leaders from around the globe and asked, "Why don't more leaders use humor?" One of the most frequent responses I hear is the fear of not being funny. No leader wants to set themselves up for failure, especially in front of his or her followers.

Well here's the good news! It is more important to SEE funny than it is to BE funny. You can be just as successful as a humor *appreciator* than as a humor *initiator*—even more so, if being funny doesn't come naturally to you. It's more important to be *authentic* than to try to be *funny* if you're not.

As a leader, being a humor appreciator means understanding that humor is a powerful tool. It means finding humor where others might not. It means encouraging humor in others. And it means creating an environment where it's safe to express one's sense of humor. It does NOT mean that you have to make people laugh. (I can hear the sighs of relief from here!)

➥ A little exercise: Appreciate the humor around you. Listen proactively for the funny things people say, even when they're not trying to be funny—like the tourist here in San Diego who asked me, "Which beach is closest to the ocean?"! Look proactively for the funny things around you, like the sign that read, "If door doesn't open, do not enter." Really?? Today, start recording these in your journal and note how much more humor you witness when you're being intentional.

A sense of humor is a desirable trait in a leader. But that's different from being funny. Be authentic. Practice *seeing* funny. Then if you *do* want to be funny, it's more likely to fall into place.

"A well developed sense of humor is the pole that adds balance to your steps as you walk the tightrope of life."

~ WILLIAM ARTHUR WARD

7
Increases Resilience

The time was one of the darkest in America's history—
The Civil War. In a meeting with his Cabinet, President
Abraham Lincoln began reading aloud from a book by
one of his favorite authors: Humorist Artemus Ward. At
the end of the chapter he laughed heartily, while his
colleagues looked upon him stonefaced. He looked at
them, put his book down and said, "Gentlemen, why
don't you laugh? With the fearful restraint that is upon
me night and day, if I did not laugh I should die, and
you need this medicine as much as I do."

One of the greatest presidents in our nation's history,
Lincoln understood the power of humor to help build

resilience. From the dour expression in most of Lincoln's portraits, you'd never know he was a great fan of humor. Yet Lincoln recognized its role in dealing with the ongoing tragedies that came as a result of a nation divided. An avid storyteller, Lincoln would tell humorous stories to put himself—and others—at ease.

During his term, Lincoln felt intense responsibility for lives lost, and he used humor to help him bear the terrible responsibility.

Lincoln didn't live long enough to see his insights into humor confirmed by modern neurological science. We now know that humor has many measurable positive effects on the mind and body.

Humor relieves anxiety and tension; it serves as an outlet for hostility and anger; it provides a healthy escape from reality; and it lightens the heaviness related to critical illness, trauma, disfigurement and death. Humor is a *healthy* coping mechanism, as opposed to the unhealthy options that many people turn to in times of extreme stress—options like alcohol, cigarettes, drugs, overeating and reckless behaviors. Humor is an excellent coping mechanism for stress management, whether that stress is short-term or long-term.

☞ A little exercise: Review the list you began creating of things that are funny to you. Then go to your calendar and schedule five-minute slots three times per week, in which to implement something humorous in your day. Make a commitment to gradually build your intervals of humor until you reach 30 minutes a day.

If you were going to run a marathon, you wouldn't wait until the day before to get in shape! (I *hope* not, anyway!) Practicing humor intentionally and consistently helps build your resilience, should you ever need to tap into this reserve during times of change, turmoil or trauma in the future.

✳

"Laughter is the shortest distance
between two people."

~ VICTOR BORGE

8

Fear of Appearing Foolish

As I chatted with Marcus, a vivacious hotel manager, I noticed that he was unconsciously rubbing his completely bald head.

"The 'Howie Mandel look' works for you," I said.

He smiled and chuckled. "Let me tell you a story.

"A few months ago I told my staff if they could go an entire month without an injury or a safety violation, I'd shave my head! I didn't really *mean* it! I was just kidding! I said it out of frustration. I didn't mean it as a *challenge*! But the staff LOVED the idea. Before you know it, for the first time in *years*, they hit the target."

"So they corner me at lunch and demand that I shave my head!" Who knew that such silliness could motivate people more than all those psychological and motivational techniques in business books?!

"My first thought was 'Oh no! I'm going to look like an idiot!' No, actually that was my *second* thought. My *first* thought was, 'My wife is gonna *kill* me'!

"But seriously, from a practical business point-of-view, I had actually accomplished two goals: Obviously, we'd met an important safety target. But the thing I hadn't expected was that this silly challenge brought my staff together in a way that I never could've anticipated! I may look ridiculous, but I suppose I'm in good company with Howie Mandel, Bruce Willis, Matt Damon and Morpheus! I just may do it again someday—after my hair grows back!"

Like Einstein said, "If you do the same thing over and over again, and expect different results, that's insanity."

Easier said than done, huh? But it's hard to change habits, risk failure, and put your reputation and professionalism on the line. (Hey, did you know that Sam Walton, founder of Wal-Mart, once lost a bet with his employees and paid-up by wearing a grass skirt and dancing the hula—down Wall Street?! But I digress.)

Most of us don't want to look silly or foolish. Actually, the word "silly" comes from an Old English term which meant to be healthy, blessed, and prosperous.

When Marcus stepped out of his comfort zone and allowed himself to appear foolish, he achieved his target—and more! As a leader, it's important to be able to stretch out of your comfort zone to achieve different and better results. Humor is a great way to do just that.

☞ A little exercise: Step out of your comfort zone today and practice a little nonsense: Belt out a silly song in front of your staff. Wear a pair of mismatched shoes. Begin your next PowerPoint presentation with a comic from "The New Yorker." Make a note in your journal about what you did, the reaction of those around you, and how you felt before and after.

Leadership involves taking calculated risks. There are no guarantees that your humor will have the desired effect. (Of course, there's no guarantee that you won't get hit by a meteorite on your way to work today. But you risked it, didn't you?) When humor is used skillfully and purposefully it usually works. And sometimes it works wonders!

"If you are too busy to laugh,
you are too busy."

~ Bob Ross

9
"Hey Everybody—Listen Up!"

I'd settled into my airplane seat (my favorite seat: Exit-row aisle...Ahh! Leg room!"). I closed my eyes and tried to meditate away all the commotion while others continued to board. Suddenly I heard someone shout: "HEY EVERYBODY—LISTEN UP!" My eyes snapped open and I glanced around. It was the flight attendant! Passengers began looking up...

She continued..."There may be '50 Ways to Leave Your Lover,' but there are only *four* ways to leave this plane!"

Now folks began chuckling—and she just kept going: "This is a non-smoking flight—but if you just *have* to have a cigarette, you may go out to our smoking section located on the wing and watch today's feature film, 'Gone With the Wind'."

People who'd ignored the safety instructions on their last 57 flights were now riveted to her every word—despite the fact that she was telling us how to put on a seat belt!!!

Just because your message contains serious information, doesn't mean you have to be dull and boring. The flight attendant was imparting serious information. But she did it through the use of humor. Why? Because she recognized that humor grabs people's attention. And because she knew that people would better remember what she had to say.

By using humor she increased their level of alertness. Neuorscience shows that people are more alert when they engage both hemispheres of their brain—and humor activates nearly all parts of the brain. By using humor she was planting visual images, or "mental hooks," in passengers' brains—and images are remembered much better than a simple narration of facts.

As a leader, you want people to pay attention to your

instructions, emails, voicemails and reports. You can anchor your information in your recipient's brain by using humor.

Your message will be fixed more firmly if your humor relates to your message. If it's just a random joke thrown into your dialogue, you may derail your listeners.

✏ A little exercise: Think of a piece of information that you want to share with your employees, audiences, customers or followers. Today, find a cartoon, humorous quote or anecdote that is in alignment with your message and figure-out several ways you could weave it in.

Humor used *strategically* enhances your communications. This is true whether you're sharing information or—as you'll soon discover—when you're negotiating or dealing with difficult people.

✳

"What I want to do is to make people laugh so that they'll see things seriously."

~ WILLIAM K. ZINSER

10

Funny Yet Serious

Picture Lucille Ball in a skit to teach the warning signs of women's heart attacks...

8:00 am — Elizabeth's morning was like every other morning—almost. A working woman with a husband, a cat, and two kids always underfoot, she was the queen of multi-tasking. She raced around feeding everyone, packing bookbags, calling in to the office. Picture the Tasmanian Devil on fast-forward.

She frowned at the sudden pain in her jaw, then ignored it. She frantically continued packing lunches—everything from acai to spaghetti. Counters were crowded with open jars, bowls and glasses, newspapers and food. Tomato sauce and peanut butter and jelly were spattered on surfaces.

Breathing heavily she clutched her chest. She popped

antacids to squelch the pain. She then scanned her coffee-stained report, and mopped sweat from her brow.

Crash! She dropped a stack of dishes. "Nobody move!" she shouted as she hastily swept up the shards.

Shen rubbed her left shoulder, trying to relieve the sudden ache.

Her 12-year-old son asked, "Are you okay mom?"

"I'm *fine*, honey," she said as a hot flash left her flushed and sweaty. "Now get ready for the carpool." She leaned on the counter as she felt dizzy.

"Mom, I think you're having a heart attack!" he said.

"Honey, do I look like the type of person who has a heart attack?" she said, smiling as she stumbled and slumped to the floor.

Her son grabbed her cellphone and pulled-up the "Warning Signs of a Heart Attack for Women." He handed her the phone. As she lay on her back holding her chest, she shouted to the kids, "I'm totally fine. Don't forget your homework! Bye!"

Elizabeth read the symptoms . "Uh-oh." Finally taking

this seriously, she called 911: "Hi! Sorry to bother you... but I think I may be having a little heart attack."

"We'll be there in two minutes."

In a panic Elizabeth leaned up, scanned the disaster in her kitchen that needed to be straightened up, and gasped, "Can you make it TEN?"

In this funny video, "Just a Little Heart Attack," featuring comic actress Elizabeth Banks, the American Heart Association conveys a serious message: Women's heart attack symptoms are *different* than men's!

And because they did it with humor, their "serious message" has gotten almost four million hits on YouTube! Can you imagine how many lives they've saved?!

☞ A little exercise: Find this video clip on YouTube and watch it all the way through. Take notes on how the serious message was conveyed through humor. How could you add one small bid of humor to a piece of information you want to communicate? You don't have to compete with Elizabeth Banks. Keep it simple for now.

Leaders need to convey serious messages—but they don't have to be solemn to be taken seriously.

✳

"There are rules for creating humor,
but unfortunately no one knows
what they are."

~ LAURENCE PETERS

11

Humor Helps Negotiations??

OCTOBER 1962 — The world held its breath as America and Russia went to the brink, with nuclear weapons at the ready. Russia was installing nuclear missiles in Cuba—a mere 90 miles from the Florida coast! The 13-day crisis played-out in real time on TV around the world.

As American and Soviet delegates came together to

Alternate chapter title: "How Humor Saved the World"

negotiate, tensions were high, and they soon became deadlocked. At one point, a Russian delegate broke the ice with a joke:

"What is the difference between Capitalism and Communism? In Capitalism, man exploits man. In Communism, it is the other way around."

Delegates on both sides laughed, and this created a bond among all of them. (Hey, ya gotta start *somewhere*!) With the tension eased for the moment, talks resumed, and eventually a deal was struck that avoided blowing up the planet—no small feat!

Whether you're negotiating for world peace or for whose turn it is to wash the dishes, humor can play a crucial role in your success.

According to a recent study on business negotiations, humor has numerous functions in the negotiation process. It can put the negotiators at ease; it can introduce a difficult issue; it can foster togetherness and team spirit; it can help the other negotiator save face; and it can be a way of being cooperative in spite of disagreement.

Additional studies show that if you can inject humor

into your negotiations, you're more likely to get what you're negotiating for.

Once when I was negotiating with a potential client over the phone, it became obvious that budget was a delicate topic. I could feel the tension rising, and when he posed the question: "How much is this going to cost me?" I wanted to reduce the tension.

I paused and said, "Are you sitting down??" He laughed, and from that point, the conversation about money went smoothly.

Those *four little words*, spoken in *just the right tone of voice*, have helped me close dozens of deals over the years.

➥ A little exercise: Who do you negotiate with? It might be with a competitor, a customer, a colleague or even a family member. (You *do* understand, I hope, that getting a child to go to bed is not something that you *command*, but rather something you *negotiate*. Some of those rugrats make Johnnie Cochran look like an amateur. And don't even get me *started* on teenagers.)

Now, regarding whatever-it-is that you negotiate for,

examine it and look for an opportunity to weave in a little humor—like a humorous-and-relevant anecdote, a funny comment or gesture. Negotiations are often important and intense. So use humor wisely, cautiously and professionally. (No "sharp jabs" like Don Rickles is famous for!) Now record your ideas in your journal.

As a leader, the ability to successfully negotiate is a valuable skill. Humor, used strategically, can make you a more powerful and effective negotiator. We will soon explore techniques that will help you become more comfortable with using humor strategically, as well as ways to avoid humor that could potentially backfire.

*

Favorite joke:

Favorite sitcom:

Favorite funny YouTube video:

Favorite family anecdote:

Most embarrassing moment:

That time when you laughed so hard
that milk spurted out of your nose:

Favorite comedian:

*"Anyone without a sense of humor
is at the mercy of everyone else."*

~ WILLIAM ROTSLER

12
Isms & Asms

"How do you drive a blonde crazy? Give her a bag of M&Ms and tell her to alphabetize them!"

"Why did the blonde put sugar in her bed? Because she wanted to have sweet dreams!"

"Why did the blonde climb a chain link fence? To see what was on the other side!"

This had become routine dinner conversation as my (former) husband recited the litany of blonde jokes he'd heard at work each day. One memorable evening my five-year old platinum blonde son's chin began to quiver and he pushed his chair away from the dinner table to leave.

My husband shouted, "Hey! Where do you think *you're* going?!"

My son turned to him, and with tears in his eyes said, "I don't like it when you make fun of me."

I smiled and reassured him, "He's not making fun of *you*, honey. 'Blonde jokes' make fun of blonde *women*, not *men*."

Adam was a little confused, but he was satisfied for the moment.

Whether at work or at home, a common humor land-mine involves what I call isms and asms. Sexism, racism, ageism, sarcasm...these jokes involve a target. Blonde jokes target blonde women—who are characterized as dumb. Racist jokes target pretty much any race in the world other than *yours*—with the message that others are inferior or outright evil. Sarcastic humor can target anyone and everyone. (FYI, the root word for sarcasm—the French word sarcastique—originally meant, "to tear the flesh." If you've ever been the target of a sarcastic remark you may have felt some hide missing!)

There are jokes making fun of older people, fat people,

uneducated people, and people in certain occupations. But before you try your hand at this kind of humor, consider these two things.

First, if you're part of the target population, it's more acceptable for you to use this kind of humor. If you're blonde, you can make blonde jokes. If you're an engineer, it's okay to joke about engineers. If you're a redneck, like Jeff Foxworthy, you can make a gazillion dollars making fun of rednecks! But if you're *not* part of the target group—always wait to be invited to participate. And if you're not... keep quiet!

Let me think of an example that won't insult *any* of you out there. Okay, here we go...

"How many speakers does it take to screw-in a light bulb? Nobody knows—they're all too busy fighting over the spotlight!"

And second, remember that if your bond with another person is *not* strong, inappropriate humor can harm or destroy that relationship. Researchers have found that people tend to believe that others have the same attitudes, priorities and beliefs that they do. In other words, we think we know people better than we actually do. This is one of the most common humor mistakes. Don't make assumptions! As a leader, your humor should be purposeful and mindful. Keep your humor constructive, and proceed with caution when using isms and asms, if you decide to use them at all.

✏ A little exercise: In your journal, write down four favorite jokes and anecdotes. Now write down who you *could* share those jokes with, and who you definitely could *not* share them with. Of *course* it's a judgment call! If you're really uncertain, here's The Rule: "When indoubt, leave it out." (I think it was Confucius who said that. Or was it Shakespeare?) Ask yourself, "Would this go over well in the company of clients, employees, colleagues, the CEO of your firm, women, blacks, Latinos, Japanese or Lichtensteiners?"

If you are not intentional, and don't consider potential landmines, humor can blow up in your face. And yet, as a leader, humor can be one of your most powerful tools to help others be more successful and happy.

✳

Off-Kilter Stuff.

_____

_____

_____

_____

_____

_____

_____

_____

_____

_____

_____

_____

_____

"As soon as you have made a
thought, laugh at it."

~ LAO TZU

13
Humor & Creativity

The small city of Hillsboro, Oregon recently needed a new Police Chief. Obviously, it was important that they attract the best candidates. But with a limited budget, how could a community their size compete with bigger cities with bigger budgets?

Enter City Manager Michael Brown—a man who isn't afraid to think outside-the-box. Instead of placing a typical job posting online, he led the way to the production of a video for YouTube that sought candidates. The creative twist was that it was a *funny* video. They used humor in the service of a serious message. Well, their video went viral and they received *loads* of applications.

Why did their video go viral? Because they did creative things like filming a mock "prisoner" in the backseat of a squad car, giving the thumbs up and saying, "I've been arrested in a lot of cities, but I gotta say the Hillsboro Police Department is top-notch!"

Integrating many short, humorous vignettes, they were able to communicate a serious message about the police force and the community—with a light touch.

But wait, *there's more!* The Hillsboro Plice Department obviously benefitted, but as an unintended consequence, the entire community was highlighted positively, the town's public image was boosted, and its residents enjoyed more civic pride.

Sometimes, wacky ideas that you'd think *wouldn't* work lead to creative solutions that actually *do* work. If you're willing to be playful, have fun and take risks, you can reap tremendous benefits.

As kids, we're naturals at creativity—and we *love* funny stuff! Creating new things is exciting and fun! But as we grow older, we're generally taught there's only ONE *right* answer to every problem. The rest are *wrong* answers—and we might even be *penalized* for creating a new answer that doesn't fit everyone's preconceived notions. We're encouraged to be serious instead of silly. And by the time we're adults, creativity no longer comes naturally to us.

☞ A little exercise: Let's give your "creativity muscle" a workout. Grab a paperclip, and in 60 seconds, write down as many different uses you can think of for it. Ready, GO! Okay, set that list aside. In the *next* 60 seconds, I want you to list the craziest, dumbest—possibly fictional—ideas you can generate. Ready, GO!

Most people's first list is somewhat creative—but practical: Pick locks. Wear as earrings. Use it as a bookmark. But many people's *second* list contains things like: Use it as a magic wand. Ride it to the moon. Play it like a musical instrument. Once you've stretched your creativity to its crazy limits, you come back to reality with a more open mind. (The creative folks in ad agencies use many exercises like these to create powerful, effective, funny or profound ads and commercials.)

Leaders are called upon to solve challenges daily. Boost your problem-solving abilities through humor and creativity.

"Humor helps us shake our heads clear, get our feet back under us and restore our sense of balance and purpose."

~ Captain Gerald Coffee

14
Detecting Humor Landmines

The nurse leader pulled me aside and said, "I feel awful! Last week I was making rounds on several hospital floors. Every time I stepped onto a unit, I could hear people snickering and giggling. But when I looked at them, they all turned away. I made sure my zipper was up and that nothing was stuck between my teeth, but whenever I asked the staff what was funny they just said, 'Oh...nothing'!

"I finally got back to my office at the end of my shift, and as I'm hanging up my lab coat I see it: A Post-It note someone had slapped onto my back! It read: 'I'm homeless and will work for food.' Normally that would have been fairly funny (in a dark sort of way)—but shortly before I had gone to my office I'd reviewed discharge plans with a destitute man and his family who had nowhere to go. I'm sure that as I turned to leave the room they had to have seen the note on my back."

She concluded, "And I promise you that you will never again see this kind of prank in our hospital."

This attempt at humor obviously was not intended for the patient and his family, but they unintentionally *became* an audience. Our humor environment includes anyone who can hear, see, or experience our humor—whether they're the intended audience or not. You might have a tight bond with the person you're sharing your humor with, but if the door is ajar and someone else hears it, they become an unintended audience. Unintended audiences are also created if someone forwards your "funny" email and someone else reads it. Or if they post your sarcastic memo in the lounge and a customer accidentally wanders into the break room and sees it.

The watchwords here are *sensitivity* and *mindfulness*.

Our humor environment might be our *physical* space or it might be *cyber* space. A young woman told me she lost her job because an off-color bit of humor she had posted on Facebook got forwarded to her manager. He felt it was unprofessional and inappropriate for an employee of their company.

As a leader, you not only need to make sure you're being cognizant of who might experience your humor, but you must also help those you are leading be more mindful about where their humor is being experienced.

☛ A little exercise: Identify an exchange of humor you've recently had via email, text or social media. Would this humor still be appropriate if you accidentally sent it to a client or your boss or your staff or your daughter—or your mother? Think about what measures you—and those you lead—can take to make sure shared humor doesn't go beyond the confines of your group. And write these down in your journal.

Like *real* landmines, *humor* landminds are initially hard to identify. But a little practice will make you a pro at spotting them well ahead of time.

✳

"You grow up the day you have
your first real laugh at yourself."

~ ETHEL BARRYMORE

15
Defusing Difficult Conversations

It was 1984, and the second presidential debate between Walter Mondale and Ronald Reagan was underway. After the first debate, critics observed that Regan looked tired, and they wondered if he might be too old for the job.

Reagan's team went to work and prepared his response. (They *knew* it was an important issue.)

Sure enough, a short while later, a reporter asked Reagan, "Given the fact that you are already the oldest president in U.S. history, would you *really* be able to function should a crisis arise?"

Reagan assured the reporter that he'd be perfectly capable of dealing with any situation at hand—and *then* he quipped—"I will not make *age* an issue of this campaign. I am not going to exploit for political purposes my opponent's youth and inexperience."

When the laughter died down, so did the question of Reagan's age. And he was elected President for a second term.

When you're engaged in a difficult conversation, people often pose what author Malcolm Kushner calls a "Hostile Question." The purpose of their question isn't really to gain information, but to challenge you, embarrass you, make you express frustration, and put you in a negative light. You might hear questions like, "Who do you think you are?!" or "Whose budget is this coming out of?!"

You have numerous ways to approach the situation. You can be serious. You can debate. You can take the situation elsewhere. You can walk away. You can BS your way out. Or you can defuse the situation with humor. All of these approaches can succeed, but determining the right choice at the right time requires some discernment on your part.

Used strategically, humor can alter the hierarchy, placing you in a more powerful position. It is a sign of confidence, and a way of taking charge. As a leader, the goal is *not* to get the other person laughing so hard that you can escape unnoticed, but to defuse tension, establish more control, and then guide the conversation in the direction that you want.

☛ A little exercise: Think back to a time when you were faced with hostile questions, particularly ones you might face again. Write down as many of these questions as you can think of. Then select one and begin creating a list of humorous responses. Come up with several. I can tell you from experience that the first few will probably be the funniest—but also the most inappropriate. (The purpose here is to defuse the bomb, not light the fuse!) As a leader, your goal is *not* to get into a power struggle, but to reach a resolution. If you practice, you'll find a response that will lightly defuse the situation and allow you to move the conversation in a more productive direction.

Whether you're dealing with irritable staff, cranky customers, or obstinate teenagers—humor is a powerful means of defusing difficult conversations.

✳

"When a person can no longer
laugh at himself, it is time for
others to laugh at him."

~ THOMAS SZASZ

16

"Someday We'll Laugh About This!"

The audience returned from a break, and I continued my presentation. But there's *always* a straggler, isn't there?

This gal tip-toed all the way down the center aisle (thinking that perhaps she wouldn't be noticed?!), then squeezed through the narrow second row (she just *had* to be in the front, of course!), bumping into a dozen people and their belongings. "Sorry!" "Sorry!" "Oops!" "Pardon me!" "Sorry!" "Sorry!"

Embarrassing, right? But wait, *there's more!* When she finally reached her seat, she went to sweep her skirt underneath her—only to discover that she'd tucked the back of her skirt into her pantyhose!

Most people would have slunk away to their hotel room, locked the door, closed the curtains, and skipped the rest of the conference. But not *her*! After my presentation she was the first person in line to talk with me. With a big smile on her face she said, "Someday I'll laugh about this, right!?" And before I could respond, she burst out laughing! She was able to detach from the pain of her embarrassment almost immediately. She had the time of her life during the rest of the conference—and she gained the respect of the group by handling her situation with humor and grace.

You can handle—or avoid—awkward situations by understanding and harnessing the TIMING of humor. Timing is an important component of humor. I'm not talking about *comedic* timing, as when Seinfeld pauses just the right amount of time before delivering his zinger of a punchline. I'm talking about the time between when you experience an embarrassing or devastating event, and when you can laugh about it. As the great Carol Burnett once observed, "Comedy is tragedy plus time."

The majority of adult humor comes from pain. Sometimes it's yours—sometimes it's someone else's. We usually don't laugh about having a *good hair day* or about *having too much money*!

When you are emotionally bound to a painful event because it feels personal, you don't have the emotional distance from it that's necessary for humor to arise. For some people it takes weeks, months or even *years* to detach from the emotion—while others can laugh immediately after an embarrassing incident. As a leader, you can avoid this humor landmine if you're mindful of how the *timing* of your humor will affect its recipient.

✍ A little exercise: Think of an embarrassing moment you have experienced in the past and write it down. Reflect on how you felt at the time. How did you feel about it a week later? Think about the amount of time you took to find it funny—if ever—and consider how the passage of time affected your emotional detachment.

You can redefine painful experiences into humorous memories if you have the right mindset, and remember that

Pain + Time = Humor

✳

"If you're not confused,
you're not paying attention."

~ TOM PETERS

17
Forklift Rodeo

It was time again for the dreaded safety certification at Cosmoflex, a plastic pipe manufacturer in the Midwest. A boring and laborious task, right? Wrong! Thanks to the ingenuity of a couple leaders, employees took part in a certification process like none before. They created "Forklift Rodeo"—and that's no bull! (Sorry, I couldn't resist the pun.)

Outside the plant, an obstacle course was laid out, involving all the necessary skills for using a forklift. Exercises included the 'Loaded Figure 8,' the 'Stack and Back,' and the ever-popular 'Ram and Jam'. (It's kind-of like parallel parking on steroids.) The safety committee judged and assigned points to the employees individually and as teams, based on their knowledge, accuracy, speed, and safety.

The initial goal was simply to complete certification for all the employees. When I asked the VP if there were any unexpected benefits he instantly said, "Yes!" He was surprised by the level of enthusiasm, the improved communications, and the contagious effect of positive attitudes.

Any downside? He smiled. "Just that the employees didn't want to return to their posts—they wanted to stay and watch their co-workers compete!"

When tasks at work are boring or laborious, people are likely to check out mentally and maybe even physically. How do you get folks to participate? The two fundamental motivators behind everything we do are pain and pleasure. So you *could* FORCE people to participate in activities by threatening them. Or you could ENTICE them by making the task more fun.

Now you may be thinking, "But you don't understand. There's no *way* you can make (fill in the blank) more entertaining." That's what most people would've said about the safety certification process at a manufacturing plant. But with some creativity and ingenuity, leaders at Cosmoflex proved them wrong. They understand that when activities include laughter and fun, people are more likely to participate willingly—and possibly enthusiastically.

☛ A little exercise: Can you think of some activities or tasks where your people tend to drag their feet? These might be tasks involving committee work, volunteerism, continuing education, or work competencies. Write these in your journal and then choose one to start playing with. How could you incorporate more humor, laughter, and fun? When you eventually implement your idea, compare the amount of participation *now* to the amount you had *before*.

When leaders use humor strategically, the benefits are abundant. Getting increased participation is a big benefit, but not the *only* one!

❋

"If we took what we now know about laughter and bottled it, it would require FDA approval."

~ Dr. Lee Berk

18

Jokes & Teasing & Pranks, Oh MY!

A restaurant in Panama City, Florida held a competition among its servers to see who could sell the most beer to their customers in a month's time—and the prize was a new Toyota!

At the end of the competition, a 26-year-old waitress had out-performed everyone. She had gone above-and-beyond anyone's expectations. She was giddy with excitement! She was taken blindfolded to the parking lot to receive her Toyota. But when the blind-fold was removed she was shocked and embarrassed to discover she had *not* won a new Toyota, but a new "toy Yoda"—a Star Wars doll. The entire staff burst out laughing. It was meant to be a harmless practical joke, but the waitress wasn't laughing. She felt that the prank was cruel, and that the contest was a sham. She quit her job and sued her employer. The amount of the settlement was undisclosed, but an attorney involved in the case revealed that the settlement would allow the young woman to buy "...*any* model of Toyota she wanted."

A *good* joke or prank can demonstrate innovation and creativity. MIT and Caltech are famous for their ingenious pranks. Students at MIT once converted the outside of the school's iconic Great Dome into a huge replica of R2D2!

Joking around at work can range from funny fake memos, to shrink-wrapping entire office cubicles, to disassembling a Volkswagen Beetle and reassembling it in the CEO's office. Apple co-founder Steve Wozniak—a big fan of pranks—believes this type of humor lends itself to the inventiveness that is essential for companies to grow and thrive.

But as a leader, when participating in a practical joke—or any kind of humor—you must ask, "Is it safe?"

Safety can be *physical* safety or *emotional* safety. Ask yourself, will a bit of humor pulled over on someone be seen as funny or cruel? Some people feel *special* knowing that the humor was planned just for them! (They enjoy being in the spotlight.) Other people might they feel targeted or bullied. (The sensitive and the shy.) Is there a chance that if something went amiss, that someone could be hurt?

Here's an observation that might help you decide if the planned joke or stunt is appropriate: If the joke would be hilarious on the sitcom "The Office," THEN DON'T DO IT!

YouTube has *thousands* of videos demonstrating pranks that left people embarrassed, humiliated or physically hurt. Successful leaders use humor to *help* people, not to *hurt* them.

✏ A little exercise: Think back to a practical joke that you participated in, either as an adult or in your youth. Reflect on what went right and what could have gone wrong. Would you still participate in that practical joke, given what you now know?

As a leader it is important that you, and those you lead, use humor constructively. Done well, it can help people—and organizations—become stronger.

✳

"When using humor to communicate information tell it serious, tell it funny, tell it serious."

~Jean Wescott

19
Improves Employee Retention

Employees of Classic Care Pharmacy gathered 'round, holding their collective breath as they waited to see who would be voted off the island. The Council spoke—and Zoe was escorted down the plank, flipped into the air—and into a wastebasket! The employees cheered, and the little plastic diorama of the Survivor TV series—complete with miniatures of Zoe and her fellow cast members—was set back up for next week's episode. Coffee break was over and everyone returned to their stations, grinning from ear-to-ear.

When I chatted with Moe Green, founder of this Canadian company, two keys to the company's success became obvious. First, Moe is a firm believer in empowering his people. Second, fun is part of the corporate culture, beginning with the interview process. If an interviewee isn't comfortable with the joking and teasing that goes on with the interview committee, then perhaps they'd be better off working elsewhere.

The weekly executive meetings include gales of laughter. "Sometimes staff will come over and close our door because we're laughing so loud," Moe admitted.

Two of their team, Judy and Girish, told me they hate to miss even a single day of work. "There's something going on every day, and most of the time it's fun!" they said.

"We don't brag too loudly to others about how good we have it here," confided another employee. "We don't want a bunch of other people vying for our jobs!"

At companies like Classic Care Pharmacy, people who come on board tend to *stay* on board. Study after study shows that the Number One reason people leave their jobs is *not* money—it is a personal conflict with a boss or supervisor. Humor improves likability. People are more likely to stick with a job—and people—

they enjoy. And when it comes time to recruit, happy employees are more likely to recommend others like themselves.

✏ A little exercise: Think about the people you're leading. How would you rate your relationship with them? How do you think they would rate *their* relationship with *you*? What kind of humor do you exchange with them? Would they recommend your organization to their colleagues or family members? Write down your thoughts in your journal.

As a leader, you can make a tremendous impact on your corporate culture using positive humor.

✳

"If I hadn't believed it,
I wouldn't have seen it!"

~ ASHLEIGH BRILLIANT

20
Believing Is Seeing

The old man clasped the visiting hospice nurse's hands and said, "Thank you! Your visits are the one thing I look forward to all week. Thank you!"

"You're very welcome, Hank," smiled his nurse, Leslie. When she opened her hands she found a $10 bill. "Wait!" she cried. "Hank, I can't take your money!"

"No, no, I insist!" he said, with tears in his eyes. "You don't know how much I appreciate you!"

Hank's wife Mary smiled and added, "You are wonderful! And we just want to give you a little gift."

Leslie brightened and said, "Okay, I'd love a gift. But not *this* gift," and she set the bill on a table.

"The best gift you could give me would be—the gift of *humor*. I love to laugh! So next week, would you gift me with a joke or funny story?"

Mary was delighted, but Hank frowned, "There's nothing funny in my life right now." Mary shot him a look. Hank said, "Okay, okay, I'll give it a try."

A week later, when Leslie returned, Hank was beaming—and he and blurted out a corny old joke as she came through the door. It was a groaner, but Hank's enthusiasm was so delightful that she laughed out loud, making Hank and Mary laugh even more.

During his treatment Hank talked about his young grandson's shenanigans, and soon the house rang with laughter.

As Leslie packed up, she said, "That was one of the best gifts I've ever received!"

"But wait—*there's more!*" Hank cried, and told her another old joke. The three of them groaned and giggled together.

As Mary walked Leslie out she whispered, "Oh, thank you, Leslie! After you left last week Hank grumped, but he started searching for humor in the newspaper funnies, and on TV—and he even got on the computer!" Mary blinked back tears and said, "He's been happier this week than I've seen him for years! Thank you for the gift of humor!"

Most people overlook the humor around them. But not me! And not Hank! And now, not *you*! Just believe and observe.

If you think nothing is funny in your life—you'll be right. But if you *think* there is humor around you and ask yourself—"What am I missing?"—you'll begin to find humor all around you.

✏ A little exercise: Throughout your day be present and ask yourself, "What funny things am I missing?" Find the absurdity in newspaper headlines and articles; find *visual* humor and *spoken* humor. Listen for both intended and unintended humor. Then record it in your journal.

Observe the world through the lens of humor. The more you do it, the easier it becomes.

✳

"The health of any organization is directly proportional to its ability to laugh at itself."

~ Bob Basso

21
Funny Means Money

A bunch of guys are playing football in a park. The ball is hiked. The quarterback steps back to throw. The receiver—an old woman—shuffles down the field. Ninety-year-old comedic actress Betty White nearly catches the ball, but she's tackled. One of her teammates yells, "Hey man, you're playing like *Betty White* out there!" She's given a Snickers Bar, which transforms her back into his proper male form. The tag line: "You're not you when you're hungry."

It became one of the most talked-about commercials in Super Bowl history.

The commercial ended, the Super Bowl returned, and

everyone hopped up to replenish drinks and take a bathroom break.

Ask folks if they watch the Super Bowl and you'll often hear, "I just watch the game for the commercials." People remember and talk about these ads! Especially the funny ones.

This is why leaders at companies like Frito-Lay, PepsiCo, Allstate Insurance, Reebok, McDonald's and Budweiser pay $4.5 million for 30-second spots, most of which are humorous. Why do they do this? Beause they understand that FUNNY MEANS MONEY.

According to Mark Levitt, professor of marketing at NYU, "People will pay more attention to a humorous commercial than a factual one, because humor undercuts logic, appeals to the emotions, and opens people to be influenced." When we find something funny, our level of alertness goes up and we retain information better. This, in turn, improves brand recognition and sales.

Just ask the folks at Taco Bell. When a tiny Chihuahua uttered the words, "*Yo Quiero Taco Bell*," the company saw a substantial rise in sales. Not only that, their mascot's phrase became part of the nation's lexicon.

This principle works for huge companies, small companies, and even individuals. The Pacific Bean, my favorite coffee shop, provides little piles of Legos at each table. The pieces have to be replaced periodically, but the owner, Peter Fillat, understands it's chump change compared to what he makes in repeat business from delighted customers.

And one president of a non-profit organization keeps her donors engaged and amused by mailing laminated cartoons to them.

✏ A little exercise: Check out funny commercials on YouTube to see what makes them work. Then look at your organization or group and start writing down how you could weave some fun into your messages.

Leaders are frequently looked upon for ways to increase revenue. So don't forget: FUNNY MEANS MONEY!

✳

"It is more important to SEE funny than it is to BE funny."

~ Karyn Buxman

22
Manipulate Your Mindset

You hop into your car and head to the office—your PowerPoint presentation tucked into your briefcase—ready to lead today's Strategic Planning meeting. On your way to work traffic slows down...then grinds to a complete halt because some fool was texting while driving and hit a fire hydrant. *Now* the street is flooded! Cars are stalled! And you are *definitely* going to be late to your meeting.

(First World Problems, right?) Maybe…

But then again, it was just one small straw that broke the camel's back. It's important to deal not only with life's major snafus, but life's minor frustrations as well.

Our brains are hardwired to be conscious of only a minute amount of the information that bombards them every second. (One estimate is that only 1/10,000th of that information is conscious to us.) The great majority of this information processing takes place at a non-conscious level. So our own unique filters determine the world that we see.

Some of us are hardwired more than others to see things from a negative or threatening point of view. This is our brain's attempt to protect us—selecting and focusing on data that could potentially harm us—but overlooking other evidence that all-is-well. Sometimes we create unnecessary stress by interpreting things to be worse than they actually are.

This is where humor can help. By twisting and turning and playing with our stress and pain, we can manipulate our mindset and see things from a different perspective.

One humorous way to manipulate your mindset during frustrating times—like getting stuck in traffic—is to exaggerate your situation mirthfully. Then exaggerate it again. And again—until you take the original situation and blow it up into such absurdity, that you can put the original event into its proper perspective. I call this "Catastrophizing."

☞ A little exercise: Let's look at our opening scenario of the World's Worst Traffic Jam: How could you catastrophize this? Well, you could've been headed to the airport to fly to the Bahamas instead of the office. How could it be even worse? You could be trapped with a car-full of screaming kids… for *hours*! How could it be *super* worse? One of the kids could have eaten a giant bean burrito just before you headed out. Uh-oh!

Ridiculous? You *bet*! But the point is that you can choose to make your situation so humungous, outrageous and absurd that you can smile—even chuckle—and recognize you were about to freak out over a minor matter.

As a leader your objectivity and ability to see things in their proper perspective enables you to make better decisions.

"Do not take life too seriously.
You will never get out of it alive."

~ Elbert Hubbard

23
Planned Spontaneity

Have you ever stayed at a W Hotel? I love them. Elegant, comfortable... and dark. Dark! Dark! Dark! The walls were black, the furniture was black, I even think the water was black—but I couldn't tell because, well, it was so DARK. But it's way cool.

I once gave a major keynote speech at a W Hotel. (And I'll let *you* guess what color the ballroom floor and the staging were.) Halfway through my talk I stepped forward to make a dramatic point...and I walked right off the front of the stage. (Picture Wile E. Coyote stepping off a cliff.)

As you might have guessed, the black carpet and the

black stage floor merged visually, leaving no hint that there was a drop-off there. (Whom do I sue??)

The audience gasped, wondering (in the dark) if I was injured; then they held their collective breath. While the stage was only three to four feet high, the fall seemed to last forever.

Thoughts swirled through my mind. Would I bust my butt? Break my neck? End-up paralyzed?

Wham! I landed flat on my back. The wind was knocked out of me, and for several moments I was unable to breathe—my mouth gaping open and closed like a fish out of water. The audience sat in stunned silence.

Being a long-time speaker, I'd maintained a death-grip on the hand-held microphone. And then I pulled out the "saver-line" that I had tucked neatly away in the back of my mind for just such an (unlikely) occasion. I sat up, looked at the audience and said, "And now I'll take questions from the floor."

The audience laughed with relief and applauded as I climbed back up onto the stage. I refused to let them see how badly I'd bruised my ego—*and* my bottom!

Some members of the audience thought I'd actually done it *on purpose*! ("Oh, she's so clever!") Good grief! But like a magician who never divulges "how it was done," I didn't tell anyone that it was "planned spontaneity" that saved my...butt.

For leaders, part of our responsibility is to anticipate and prepare for what could go wrong. You obviously can't anticipate *every* possibility, but you *can* anticipate the most *probable* ones.

When you make a mistake, humor can be the saving grace. I'm not saying you should just laugh off a serious mistake. However, when used mindfully, humor will decrease the tension, acknowledge the error, and provide some comic relief. Done well, it can also show you have the ability to laugh at yourself.

If you listen carefully to successful comics and politicians, you'll begin to hear the saver-lines they pull out after a snafu. They've thought ahead and crafted a clever answer should the need arise.

☛ A little exercise: Today, start a list of the possible—*and* the *probable*—mistakes, glitches, problems, interruptions or Freudian slips that you might experience.

Then write a list of comebacks you hear others use. As you develop your own potential saver-lines, pair them with your possible blunders. Practice the lines aloud—the goal is to get them well-planted into your subconscious mind. So when the need arises, your response will come of its own accord, and appear to be spontaneous.

(You know, I think I'm breaking some kind of Speaker Secret Code of Honor by revealing to you this technique. Shhh, let's just keep this betweeen you and me, okay??)

Mistakes happen. As a leader, you can plan ahead and use humor strategically to acknowledge a problem and bounce right back.

*

THIS PAGE INTENTIONALLY LEFT BLANK.

"What is unspeakably irritating today may well be tomorrow's funny story. So have a good laugh today!"

~ Nancy Comiskey

24
Manipulate Your Environment

"The inbound plane is still in Baltimore. Once it's airborne we will be able to give you a more accurate departure time." All of us waiting at Gate 34 at JFK Airport groaned. The chances of making connections to our final destinations were between slim and none.

When we finally boarded—two and a half hours later—I was tired, grumpy and near tears. I was going to miss dinner with my client, arrive way past midnight, and could already picture just how exhausted I would be the next morning when it was time to take the stage.

The cabin door closed. Absolutely miserable, I pulled

out my smart phone, scanned my playlist, and turned on "David Sedaris Live at Carnegie Hall."

As he narrated a ridiculous story about his sister's parrot, a smile crept across my face. He then told a tale about the curious fact that blind people can get hunting licenses in Michigan. (It's *true*. Look it up!) I chuckled quietly. He also told tales about how Santa in the *Netherlands* is different from Santa in *America*. (For example, while America's Santa gives *coal* to naughty kids, the Netherlands' Santa might "...pretend to kick you and beat you, stuff you into a sack, and take you to Spain.") I laughed so hard, tears rolled down my cheeks. The flight attendant walking by mistook my laughter for crying and tried to console me. I *really* lost it.

Often, when we're most in need of humor, odds are it won't be handy. By manipulating your environment, you can stack the deck in your favor and increase the likelihood of humor occurring in your day. This might mean manipulating your physical environment. Some of the enlightened companies I've worked with encourage their employees to express themselves through their cubicles. Thus you'll find cartoons and posters and photos and bobble-heads and balloons and Play-Doh and Barbies in various work spaces.

In addition to your *physical* environment, It might be your *cyber*-environment that needs manipulation. There are tons of apps available for your phone or tablet that provide a steady stream of humor. You can create playlists of your favorite funny podcasts, authors or radio shows. You can bookmark humorous pages on YouTube, Facebook, and other social media sites. If you're a traveler, you'll want to be sure you download some of these onto your iPad, computer, or smart phone. With today's technology, humor need never more than a click away.

✏ A little exercise: What can you change in your environment to keep humor readily accessible? Today, write in your journal *one* thing that you can alter in your physical environment, plus one new website you can visit for a dose of humor. Commit to making your change in the next 48 hours.

There are times when it seems like there's absolutely nothing funny happening in your life. Prepare for these times by strategically stacking the deck in your favor. Create an environment that increases the likelihood you'll experience humor.

✳

"It's amazing how much we can do if we don't care who gets the credit."

~ HARRY S. TRUMAN

25
"Look at ~~Me~~! <u>You</u>!"

The Second City improv troupe in Chicago took their bows to the cheering crowd, then came off stage. I grabbed my son, Adam, by the arm and headed to a restaurant to feed my starving artist and budding comedian. Twenty-three years old and an aspiring improv student, he paid his bills waiting tables.

As he gulped down the biggest sushi roll I'd ever seen, I asked him, "You're a real talent on stage, but if 'Saturday Night Live' doesn't discover you, will this improv stuff ever help you earn real money?"

His answer surprised me. "Mom, I always get better tips than the other waiters because I'm funny. But since I've studied improv, I've learned that one of its first Rules is to 'Make the other guy look good.' You see, if everybody helps everybody else, you create the best show.

"So as a waiter I started looking at the customers at my tables as members of my troupe, and I realized that at every table there's someone who thinks *they're* funny too.

"Mom, when *I'm* funny I get good tips! But when I can *make that other person look funnier than me*—I get *amazing* tips!"

Improv is one of my favorite resources for humor. But it wasn't until Adam explained that rule to me that I realized improv gives you options, opportunies and creative responses that simply would never come about otherwise.

"Make the other guy look good." This great improv rule works as well—or better—off the stage! As a leader, it's important to model good behavior. But sometimes our egos may get in the way of our objectives. If the message you're communicating (intentionally or not) is "Look at me! Look at me!" your followers will probably feel disengaged, unappreciated, and they may judge you to be a show-off.

✏ A little exercise: Think of someone on your team who might benefit from positive attention. How could you make that happen in a humorous, non-threatening way at your next meeting? How could you, or another member of the team, help this person shine? Write down your thoughts and then take action.

As a leader, it's not just about *you* looking good. It's about making those you lead look good, too. If your people follow your lead and start making *others* look good, you'll raise productivity and morale across the board. (And, so I've heard, great productivity and positive morale are two important factors that lead to profitability! But maybe that's just a rumor.)

✳

"A person without a sense of humor
is like a wagon without springs—
jolted by every pebble in the road."

~ HENRY WARD BEECHER

26
Set the Tone

The *voice* was that of pop singer Pharrel Williams but the *face* was that of Dr. Bob Dent, Senior VP and COO of a highly successful hospital in Texas. And the nurses were howling at the YouTube video that their colleagues had created to help them celebtate National Nurses Week. Bob was lip-synching the popular song "Happy," and other leaders and staff members were dancing and clapping and in general making fools of themselves to bolster the spirits of their nurses.

Bob's full title is Dr. Bob Dent, DNP, MBA, RN, NEA-BC, CENP, FACHE. But just because he has more letters *behind* his name than *in* his name, doesn't mean he takes himself too seriously. Quite the contrary. Whether it's poking fun at himself or being playful with his employees, Bob's caring, compassion and charisma are expressed through his sense of humor.

Bob told me, "When we look at engagement levels and patient satisfaction scores we see that the use of humor has a positive impact." He added, "We're always striving for balance. There's a time to be serious and a time to have fun. The result is an environment where there's both fun *and* productivity."

Whether it's bringing in balloons and cinnamon rolls to celebrate achievements, or dumping ice water on his head for charity, Bob looks for opportunities to set the tone for fun and celebration.

Bob participated in "The Ice Bucket Challenge" in 2014, which raised millions of dollars to find a cure or prevent ALS (Lou Gehrig's Disease). Bob entertained his hospital staff and patients by meeting the Ice Bucket Challenge outside, in front of the hospital!

Setting the tone for humor means leading by example. It means encouraging and supporting your followers. It means creating a welcoming and fun environment.

Want to be bold? Follow the lead of companies like Zappos, Mercedes Benz, Southwest and LinkedIn. They've actually worked "sense of humor" or "fun" into their mission, vision, or values. These companies recognize that setting the tone for humor and fun improves engagement, productivity and morale. (Oh, and by the way, it improves their bottom lines!)

You don't have to go this alone. Whenever possible, involve others in creating the tone. You'll get more ideas, more ownership and more involvement. And if one person has to drop out of the mix, the momentum can continue.

✏ A little exercise: Reflect on your current company culture. What's one step you could take to increase the humor? Who else could you get involved?

Great leaders set the tone for humor by their own actions and by encouraging the actions of others.

✳

"More than any other element,
fun has been the secret
to Virgin's success."

~ RICHARD BRANSON

27
Create a Humor Habit

As Jamie cruised through the hospital, he raised his right hand and called out, "High Five Friday!" The staff laughed, and one by one, everyone gave him a high five, and called back, "High Five Friday!"

At 6'8" Jaimie Veach, the COO, is hard to miss. His quick smile and willingness to express genuine enthusiasm created an uplifting feeling that most people found irresistible. A youthful-looking forty-something, he already had almost 20 years of leadership experience under his belt. As we chatted, he seemed wise beyond his years. I asked him what was behind "High Five Fridays."

"We become what we surround ourselves with," he explained. "When I first started working here, the negative energy was palpable." It was especially quiet during my rounds one Friday. So I just decided to liven things up a bit! It didn't take long for 'High Five Fridays' to catch on and spread! Not just with the staff, but with patients and even their families. They were even high-fiving each other. This silly routine helped us create a culture of fun, friendliness and openness."

There are many pieces to the puzzle that make up an organization's culture, but an often overlooked puzzle piece is routine. Not as in a, "*boring* routine"—but as something done regularly over a long period of time. Habits are unconscious behaviors, while routines are usually consciously chosen behaviors.

Jaimie understands that humor has the power to strengthen relationships and improve the corporate culture. He also understood that these benefits could be leveraged on a routine basis. When humor happens by *chance* it's *entertaining*—but when humor happens by *choice*, it leads to *results*.

Now *here's* something that may surprise you: Humor works not only *while* it's happening, but also *before* it happens. How can *that* be? Because of something called the Anticipatory Response.

Neuroscience has shown that when people anticipate something/anything, they "prepare" for it psychologically, emotionally and physically. The anticipated "something" could be good or bad or painful or joyful or frightening or funny. Specific research has been conducted on the effects of humor, and the Anticipatory Response is powerful in the realm of Funny Stuff.

When we know that something humorous is about to happen, we get many of the same benefits as if the event were actually occurring. So by setting the stage for humor, you're getting a double-bang for your buck: When your people begin to anticipate the humor AND when the event actually occurs.

☞ A little exercise: Think about the routines that take place within your organization. Write in your journal one way you could strategically schedule humor into one or more of these activities.

There are simply too many benefits to let humor happen by chance. As a leader you can make humor happen by *choice* by creating fun routines, setting the stage, setting expectations, and by walking the talk.

✳

"As a leadership skill,
humor must be taken seriously."

~ Scott Davis

28
Walk the Talk!

After I took a bow at the end of my presentation for a leadership retreat, the CEO came up to me and said, "That was incredible! This is exactly what our people need to hear! We want you to come back and address *everybody* in our system—from middle management to housekeeping. Our surveys tell us they're good at their jobs, but their attitudes are negative and morale is terrible. They all need to hear just how powerful humor can be for them and our patients."

Wow! A speaker's favorite phrase is "Back by popular demand!" And so, six weeks later, I returned, and over the course of *three* days spoke *nine* times to more than *one-thousand* employees. It was a party, it was a love fest. Staff from every department responded to the message whole-heartedly. I was over the moon! (Speakers *love* it when our messages are embraced!). But something unexpected and troubling arose from the audience's evaluations of my presentation.

Again and again I read, "This was *really* helpful. I just wish my BOSS could have heard it." Huh?! It was the BOSS who had brought me in!

I then realized that *none* of the top leadership had attended *any* of my *nine* presentations over the past *three* days. Granted, they'd already heard the message, *but the staff didn't know that.* And in the six weeks since my work with the leaders at the very top of the organization, there apparently hadn't been any trickle down, in terms of modeling behavior. Reflecting on the lack of communication and visibility of their leadership—at least from the employees' point of view—the low morale was no surprise.

Ralph Waldo Emerson said, "Your actions speak so loudly, I can not hear what you are saying." This organization's leaders told me they believed in the importance of humor for themselves and their people, but their *behavior* was communicating to the staff,

"Firings will continue until morale improves!" And since there was no visibility of leadership at the staff presentations, there was no indication that there was buy-in from the top.

Your message and your actions *have* to be congruent. When using humor in your leadership role, this goes beyond "giving permission" for others to express humor. People are looking at *you* to be a role model. It's vital that you walk the talk.

☞ A little exercise: How can you demonstrate authentically that you believe humor is not only acceptable, but *encouraged*? It's important to choose a humor style that fits you, and then use it purposefully. Write down five ways you could model humor appreciation, and then choose one that you can begin to implement over the next several days.

Leaders, your followers are looking to you for guidance. Model behavior by *choice*, not by *chance*. Humor is a powerful tool for you and those you lead. We've covered many ways to model this message, from subtle to outrageous. Next we'll talk about the secret messages people hide in some of their humor.

✳

"Humor is the affectionate
communication of insight."

~ LEO ROSTEN

29
Beyond the Laughter

"I feel like a one-armed paper hanger!"

"Yesterday I turned away from my little boy, and when I turned back he was in college!"

"I'm great at diets! I've defeated seven of them in the last year alone!"

Three humorous comments. But might there be a message-behind-the-humor?

Let's listen more closely…

"I feel like a one-armed paper hanger!" This might be idle chatter at work. Or it might be a safe way of saying

"I'm too darned busy! I'm overwhelmed! This job is killing me."

"Yesterday I turned away from my little boy, and when I turned back he was in college!" This might simply be a humorous observation that life really does fly by. Or it might be code for, "My family is suffering because I work too late."

"I'm great at diets! I've defeated seven of them in the last year alone!" This might be just a little self-deprecating humor. Or it might be a safe way of letting people know that, "I feel embarrassed about the way I look. And my self-esteem is really suffering."

How can you know for sure what the real message is? You listen...really listen. Listen between the lines. Listen beyond the humor. When you really pay attention, you're more likely hear what's *really* being communicated.

It takes some conscious effort, but it doesn't really take any more time! "A manager who listens to me" is cited as a top quality that employees want in a boss. Great leaders listen...on more than one level. And then—they take action.

I don't mean that you should say, "Hey, Sally! What's up with your fat-jokes?" Sometimes "taking action" simply means paying more attention to Sally, to see what you pick-up over a few weeks. Sometimes "taking action" means sitting down with Sally and giving her the space to open up, and the reassurance that you really care.

Other times, the best action is to share your concerns with your human resources expert. Of course, sometimes a joke's just a joke. But sometimes it's a call for help.

✏ A little exercise: Over the next week, be more present. Listen closely to the humor expressed by those around you. Can you identify an example where someone has used humor to test the water to see if it's safe? Write about it in your journal.

One important skill of a good leader is the ability to be aware and present, even in your humor. Doing so will help you do a better job of helping others. This and the other skills you've learned will take your leadership abilities to a new level.

❋

"True Success is not measured in dollars and cents, but in the moments that you live amazed and amused."

~ KARYN BUXMAN

30
Humor Is Power

After I concluded my keynote speech "Humor Is Power," dozens of people lined-up to share their experiences with me and ask questions. One gentleman shook my hand and asked, "Have you *always* been this funny?"

Surprisingly, in my 25 years as a speaker, no one had *ever* asked me that. "You know, I've never really thought about it...I guess so." But a week later, while visiting my mother and recounting the great response I had gotten from this audience, I recalled the gentleman's question.

"Hey Mom—have I *always* been funny?"

She cocked her head thoughtfully and said, "No."

I have to admit I was taken aback! And when she saw

my surprise, she smiled and added, "But you always had a sunny disposition."

Who knew?! I mulled that over for some time and then realized that once I became a true student of humor—in graduate school—and I saw just how beneficial humor could be, I became determined to bring more humor into my everyday life. I became willing to take more risks, because the advantages of humor far outweighed the disadvantages. Once I started practicing SEEING funny, the BEING funny fell into place naturally. This is now my life's work, and I will forever be a student of humor.

Congratulations. You, too, have become a student of humor—you've read this whole darn book! Thank you, I am honored. I hope it has been worth your time, and that you will act on the ideas and suggestions that ring true for *you*.

You now know that humor can be used to build people up, or tear them down. You have in your toolbox many ways to keep your humor positive. You have the ability to recognize and avoid humor landmines. You have at your disposal a tool that will build resilience, enhance communication, and boost engagement.

And you can use this tool any*time* you choose, any-*where* you choose.

Leading with laughter is a skill, and like all skills, the more you practice it the better you get at it, and the easier it becomes. Practice doesn't really make *perfect*—but it *does* make *permanent*. So like other skills, you don't want to just practice it consistently, but correctly.

✏ A little exercise: Review your journal, reflect on what you've learned. Celebrate your accomplishments! And set new intentions for what you will actually imple-ment—over the next 30 days, the next six months, the next year.

You are now taking your place among the many pow-erful and successful leaders who recognize that *humor is power*. And as Uncle Ben said to Peter Parker (Spiderman), "With great power comes great respon-sibility." Please use your newly-acquired power wisely, and continue to lead with laughter!

Yours in laughter *Karyn*

Humor Resources
Tools for Creating Your Humor Habit

www.aath.org Association for Applied and Therapeutic Humor (AATH) For those who practice positive humor in your professional and/or personal life. Annual conference with CEUs and graduate credit; articles; teleseminars/webinars and more.

www.Avanoo.com/KarynBuxman "Lead with Levity! A Strategic Tool for Leaders" is a 30-day online program, 3 minutes a day of checking in, watching a video, and setting an intention.

www.Beyond-Funny.com Improving brain health, as well as raising awareness and providing support for those dealing with Alzheimer's (caregiver or patient) through humor and laughter.

www.LevityWorks.com Articles, videos, resources from thought leaders around the country on humor as a strategy for peak performance and optimum health.

www.WorldLaughterTour.com A plethora of information about therapeutic laughter (also known as laughter for no reason!).

Bio

Karyn Buxman

Karyn Buxman, RN, MSN, CSP, CPAE is an international speaker, successful author, and neurohumorist.* Karyn is a pioneer in the field of applied humor, starting with her masters thesis on "Humor, Health and Communication," and continues her partnerships with leading neuroscientists. Today Karyn helps leaders—and those they serve—achieve peak performance and optimum health through the art and science of applied humor.

More than 500 organizations—including NASA, the Mayo Clinic, the Million Dollar Roundtable and Cigna—have hired Karyn to entertain, educate and inspire their people again and again. Along with Ronald Reagan and Les Brown, Karyn is one of 227 people in the world—and one of only 39 women—to be inducted into the prestigious Speaker Hall of Fame. Karyn's mission is to improve global health and business through laughter—and heal the humor-impaired.

* Neurohumorist: One who studies the intersection of humor and the brain.

Sign-Up for Free Bonus Materials!

www.KarynBuxman.com/Leadership

Articles

Tips

Research

Videos

Blogs

Podcasts

and

Prizes Of Unspeakeable Value

Made in the USA
Charleston, SC
11 September 2016